Write Now!

by
Paul Fleisher

illustrated by Corbin Hillam

Cover by Corbin Hillam

Copyright © Good Apple, Inc., 1989

ISBN No. 0-86653-493-8

Printing No. 987654

GOOD APPLE, INC.
BOX 299
CARTHAGE, IL 62321-0299

TABLE OF CONTENTS

INTRODUCTION

Even with the advent of computers and satellite communications, writing skills are as important as ever. Most of the information flashing around our planet at the speed of light still originates as written words. New technologies have helped create a world in which more printed material is being published than ever before. And people still want to express themselves through essays, stories, poems and plays. Despite the fears of some educators, the need for our students to become capable writers is greater than ever.

The activities in *Write Now!* were developed in my own classroom during the past eighteen years. I hope they will give your students many productive hours and help them develop both their writing skills and a sense that writing is a satisfying means of self-expression. If you present them to your students with a dash of enthusiasm and your own belief that good writing is important, I believe they'll work as well for you as they have for me.

In designing and constructing the activities in this book, I've tried to keep four principles in mind:

I. Editing and rewriting is an essential part of the writing process. Students resist this part of writing, but if we insist upon it, they come to accept rewriting as inevitable and even begin to see its value. Using the acronym CARE (Change, Add, Rearrange and Eliminate) should help students remember what they should do as they rewrite, and give them a simple way to manage what must often look like an overwhelming job that must be done after they think they've already finished.

Teachers shouldn't hesitate to suggest ways for students to correct or improve their writing—professional editors work that way with professional writers after all. By serving as editor, teachers show respect for students'

work and also model the behaviors and attitudes they want students to develop as they learn to revise their own work independently. Editing also helps students produce polished work, work which breeds student pride and satisfaction.

II. Organization and structure help students build a good piece of writing. Students don't suffer from a shortage of ideas, but organizing their thoughts in "permanent" form on paper can be a daunting task. This is particularly true in poetry writing. Children are often confused about how to construct a poem. They are not sure about how or where to start, what to include, and even what kinds of

GA1088

words to use. Clearly structured assignments, with specific step-by-step instructions, help circumvent this problem.

The same principle holds true for writing prose. Young writers need help putting their ideas and images into a logical structure. Many of the activities in this book could be considered "prewriting" activities, in that they are intended to help students define and organize their thoughts coherently. Once that has been accomplished, creating a final written product comes much more easily.

III. Student writing should be "real" and not just an exercise. By that I mean that students should know that they're not just practicing their skills for some unspecified future time or writing just for a grade. They should write for a genuine purpose whenever possible. Students can write **real** letters and actually mail them. They can submit their stories and essays to student newspapers and literary magazines. At the very least, they should know that their work **will** be read by others.

Writers write so that others will read what they've written. Each assignment should have built into it some method of sharing the final results. Many of the pages in this book end with an additional activity that uses the students' final products. For the others, it's essential to provide an audience by giving students the opportunity to read their work aloud or posting it on a bulletin board. When students know that their work will be read by classmates and others, their motivation to do their best is much higher. And they'll get valuable, instructive feedback from their readers, too.

IV. Students should have fun when they write. Assignments need not be deadly serious in order to teach writing skills. I've tried to make the activities in this book good-humored, entertaining and thought-provoking. Poets, essayists and novelists find joy in the sounds and rhythms of words and in saying exactly what they mean, in precisely the right way. Student writers can experience some of that same pleasure, and so can writing teachers. I hope that teachers will participate along with their students in many of the activities in this book. So have fun and enjoy *Write Now!*

Many of the ideas in this book are not completely original. Teachers are notorious scavengers. We appropriate good ideas wherever we find them and modify them for our own purposes. I want to thank Gregg Neylan, Susan Stebbins, Donna Fout, and my wife Debra Fleisher for contributing ideas that have taken form in this book. I wish I could acknowledge *all* my other colleagues who, directly or indirectly, provided the seeds from which these activities grew, but my memory is inadequate to the task. I've simply met too many teachers willing to share their good ideas—or the good ideas they'd borrowed from others—during the past eighteeen years. Nevertheless, I feel a powerful debt of gratitude to them and to the spirit of sharing and cooperating that infuses our profession.

GA1088

TAKE CARE OF YOUR WRITING

No writing is finished after just one draft (copy). To make it good, you have to rewrite it. Rewriting is **not** just recopying. You have to find all the places where you can make your writing better and change what you've written.

Professional writers rewrite over and over again. Every word must be exactly right before a writer decides a story or poem or article is finished.

If you are going to do your best writing, you'll have to rewrite too. Before you turn in an assignment, read over what you've written. Find places where you need to make improvements. It's the **only** way to write something that is truly your best work.

Here's an easy guide to help you remember what to do when you rewrite. Just remember to CARE for your writing.

CARE stands for:
> Change—a word you've written to a better word
> Add—new ideas and details
> Rearrange—the order of your words or sentences
> Eliminate—mistakes and unnecessary words or ideas.

Here is an example of each step.

Change: Sue ~~laughed~~ giggled when the ~~dog's~~ puppy's tail touched her cheek.

Add: The puppy was (tiny and) brown. (He had big, friendly eyes.)

Rearrange: Sue had never seen such a cuddly, (cute) dog (in all her life).

Eliminate: She wanted the little cocker spaniel more than anything else in the world ~~she had ever wanted.~~

CAREing for your writing will make a big difference. Your writing **will** be better!

- -

Fold the top of your paper down to this line.

Can you remember what the letters in CARE stand for? Let's see. Remember, each one is something you should do when you revise your writing.

C stands for _____

A stands for _____

R stands for _____

E stands for_____

GA1088

TAKE CARE OF YOUR WRITING

The C in CARE stands for CHANGE. There can be many different ways to say any one idea. A good writer tries to find the **best** way.

For example, suppose a character in your story **looked** out a window. You might want to change that word to "stared," or "peeked," or "peered," or "glared," or "glanced." It would all depend on what was happening in the story. Each word would give your story a slightly different meaning, so it's important to choose just the right one.

After you've written your first draft (copy), read it over carefully. Look for words that should be changed—changed to other words that will make your writing more interesting, or say what you mean more exactly.

Let's practice changing some words. In each sentence below, change the word(s) in bold to make the sentence more interesting and exciting.

1. Bob **ran** up the path to his house.
2. "I never want to see you again," Jill **said**.
3. The **animal** howled at the moon.
4. "Aren't you finished yet?" David **said**.
5. Mr. Edwards turned his car onto the **road**.
6. I **don't like** your new haircut.
7. The tiger **moved** through the jungle.
8. It was the strangest **thing** my family had ever seen.
9. That certainly is a **big** box.
10. "**Wow**," Cynthia shouted.

For these sentences, find a word that you want to change. Make each sentence more interesting, more specific or more descriptive.

1. The fire began to burn out of control.
2. "I don't believe you one bit," Nancy said.
3. Mr. White came into the room with an interesting machine.
4. The tall, strong athlete ran around the track.
5. She heard a scary sound that came from somewhere in the dark woods.

GA10

TAKE CARE OF YOUR WRITING

The A in CARE means ADD. Sometimes you may leave important ideas out of your first draft. Sometimes you leave out small details that would make your writing more interesting. When you CARE, look for places where you can ADD to what you've written. You might ADD just a word or two. You may ADD a whole sentence—or even more.

Remember, people can't read your mind. If you want them to know what you're thinking, tell them. You have to write it down! So check your writing for places where you've left something out—places to ADD something that makes your ideas clearer.

Try to make each of the sentences below more interesting by adding **at least** one more word or phrase.

1. Walter slammed the door and ran to his room.

2. Mrs. Fowler opened her shop at ten o'clock on Saturday.

3. The craft landed on the lawn.

4. Dennis knew that he was in trouble.

5. Snow covered all the houses and trees.

3

TAKE CARE OF YOUR WRITING, PART II

Now read this simple story.

Jane wanted a dog.

One day she looked outside and saw a puppy.

He was lost.

Jane went outside and made friends with the dog.

She took it inside and fed it.

Her mother asked where the dog came from.

Jane told her.

Jane's mother said she could keep the little dog.

Jane was very happy.

This story needs more details!

ADD a new sentence between each sentence that's already there, to make the story better.

TAKE CARE OF YOUR WRITING

The R in CARE means REARRANGE. The order of words in a sentence is important. Look at these two sentences, for example:

Driving down the highway, Laura saw a moose.
Laura saw a moose driving down the highway.

Both sentences have exactly the same words. But they are arranged differently, so they have different meanings. Some sentences sound stronger if you rearrange them.

The heavy container was lifted by two burly men.
Two burly men lifted the heavy container.

Most people would say that the second sentence is much better.

The order of ideas and events is important too. Many stories are told in the order that the events happen. Here's a short example.

The masked man quietly pushed the door open. He turned the doorknob slowly, so it wouldn't make a sound.

And here's the same sentences, REARRANGED so the events are in order.

The masked man turned the doorknob slowly, so it wouldn't make a sound. Then he quietly pushed the door open.

Rearrange the following sentences and short paragraphs to make them sound better or make more sense.

1. With a crashing sound, Jim heard the bowling ball hit the pins.

2. The thief died, and he was shot by the bank guard.

3. How would you let someone know you have a problem? Knowing how to write letters is important. Suppose you had a complaint about a product you bought. And a letter lets you keep a record of your complaint. A letter to the company that made the product usually gets quick action.

4. On the grill, Mr. Jackson cooked a thick, juicy steak.

5. The trapper lit the pile of firewood. Gathering the wood was hard work. It was very cold. Without a fire, the trapper knew he might freeze. His hands were stiff and painful. Finally he had collected enough for a campfire.

6. The nurse put a Band-Aid on his finger, pulled the splinter out, and swabbed it with alcohol.

7. Mrs. Wilson had a good day. She got a raise at work, won a million dollars in the state lottery, saw an old friend she hadn't talked to in months, and heard her favorite song on the radio.

8. The letter was ten minutes late. It was delivered by a messenger at eleven thirty.

5

Student Work Sheet

TAKE CARE OF YOUR WRITING

The E in CARE stands for ELIMINATE errors. Your first draft will probably have spelling, grammar and punctuation mistakes. When you CARE for your writing, one of your jobs is to find those errors and ELIMINATE them.

Papers that don't have mistakes show that you're proud of your work.

Sometimes a first draft also has words, or even whole sentences, that aren't needed. They don't add anything to what you've written. Maybe you've repeated yourself. Or maybe you've written something that doesn't fit with the rest of your story or poem. When you rewrite your work, you should also ELIMINATE those unnecessary words. For example:

Charlie was really, ~~really~~ angry. He had never been treated so badly before. ~~He was mad.~~ How could they have done this to him?

Read the sentences and short paragraphs below. Eliminate all spelling errors, grammar errors, and unnecessary words.

1. "I used to think I would never like to ate fish the old sailer said.

2. The tired old siamese cat, who was very old, curled up on the carpet and purred softly.

3. "My brother never makes misteaks." Bennie bosted. "Hes perfect."

4. Ralph drew a big, huge picture of a anteloupe running across a grassy plane.

5. "Did you see this mornings newspaper," Mrs. Bolton asked? "The Mayor has resigned!"

In each paragraph below, find an unnecessary sentence that can be eliminated.

6. Walter needed to build a doghouse. His dog, Busby, was getting too big to sleep inside. Walter's cat slept underneath the kitchen table. When Busby jumped up on the bed, Walter could feel the springs getting ready to give way. And when he started growling in his sleep in the middle of the night, he woke up the whole family.

7. Matson opened his briefcase and looked inside. It was empty! The briefcase was made of the finest leather. The handcuffs that linked his wrist to the handle of the case were still locked securely. It hadn't been out of his sight all day, but somehow, the papers had been removed!

8. Mrs. Jones looked at her garden proudly. Everything was growing beautifully. The corn stalks were already six feet tall, and she could see the orange tops of carrots peeking out of the ground. Carrots are a good source of vitamin A. The first tomatoes were beginning to turn red, and the cabbages were just about ready to pick. Yes, it looked like it would be a good harvest.

GA1088

TAKE CARE OF YOUR WRITING
DO-IT-YOURSELF CARE WORK SHEET

Now that you know how to take CARE of your writing, you should be able to make a work sheet for someone else to answer. You'll write some sentences that need improvements. Then someone else in your class will have to fix them.

1. Write a sentence with a word or words that could be CHANGED to make the sentence better.

_____

_____

2. Now write another one.

_____

_____

3. Write a sentence which needs some words or ideas ADDED to it.

_____

_____

4. Write another.

_____

_____

5. Write a sentence which needs to be REARRANGED.

_____

_____

6. And a second one.

_____

_____

7. Write a sentence which has some errors that should be ELIMINATED. _____

_____

_____

8. Write one more.

_____

_____

Exchange papers with a classmate, and CARE for each other's sentences.

GA1088

Poster

TAKE CARE OF YOUR WRITING

Say exactly what you mean . . .

CHANGE

    to a better choice of words

        ugliest

        ~~most unattractive~~

She was wearing the ~~worst~~ hat I had ever seen!

GA1088

Poster

TAKE CARE OF YOUR WRITING

ADD

Luis $\wedge$ sat down at the piano and began playing some $\wedge$ soft, jazzy music.

9

GA1088

TAKE CARE OF YOUR WRITING

REARRANGE

Scampering through the blackberry bushes, Doris saw three baby rabbits.

GA108

Poster
TAKE CARE OF YOUR WRITING

ELIMINATE ERRORS . . .

      slammed   brakes   !

Agent 704 ~~slamed~~ on the ~~breaks~~, sending the car into a dangerous skid~~?~~

. . . AND UNNECESSARY WORDS

The car spun towards the edge of the cliff. ~~It was really dangerous~~!

11

GA1088

ONE-LINERS

If your students are like most kids, they love to tease and insult one another. Here's an introductory poetry activity which will let them engage in some good-natured insults, which aren't directed at anyone in particular. It's sure to tickle your students' funny bones while they write.

Start by writing a class poem or two. Give each student a strip of paper. Write the question "How weird was he?" on the board. Have students write the words "He was so weird . . ." on their paper, and then complete their thoughts with one-liners such as you might hear on the *Tonight Show*. When everyone is finished writing, collect the strips of paper. Shuffle them and put them together in a stack. Then read them back to the class as a single piece of writing.

Repeat the process again with the question "How ugly was she?"

Once the class has the idea, pass out copies of the following page, ONE-LINERS, PART II. Have each student write his own poem, with at least four to six "one-liners," that all respond to the same question.

If students have trouble finding an adjective to write about, here are some suggestions to get them started.

How stupid was he/she?   How mean was he/she?
How foolish was he/she?   How short was he/she?
How tall was he/she?   How fat was he/she?
How rude was he/she?   How angry was he/she?
How slow was he/she?   How careless was he/she?
How selfish was he/she?   How dirty was he/she?

If you'd rather write about more positive virtues, try some of these:

How smart was he/she?   How handsome (beautiful) was he/she?
How polite was he/she?   How clever was he/she?
How strong was he/she?   How fast was he/she?
How friendly was he/she?   How careful was he/she?
How thoughtful was he/she? How gentle was he/she?

Or make up your own! Remember, emphasize that students are writing about an **imaginary** person. Let's make sure no one's feelings get hurt!

GA1088

ONE-LINERS, PART II

You've written a couple of one-liner poems as a class. Now you can write one of your own.

Put an interesting adjective in the blank in the question below.

How _____ was he/she?

Now decide whether you want to write about a "he" or "she."

Now let's write a one-liner poem. Start each answer with He/She was so _____. Think of AT LEAST five different answers to your question. DO NOT USE RHYMES!

_____

_____

_____

_____

_____

_____

_____

_____

Can you change any of the words you used to make your poem even better? CAREfully recopy your poem on a clean sheet of paper.

GA1088

SWEET ADD-A-LINE POETRY

Sweet add-a-line poetry is an unthreatening way to get students writing verse. It makes a good way to introduce a poetry unit or a quick, fun writing activity at any time.

Here's how to do it: Each student writes **any** interesting subject for a poem at the top of his page. Tell students not to worry about actually writing the poem—other people will do that. That will free them to think of a wider range of creative topics.

If a few students have difficulty coming up with a title, suggest any of the following general categories:

Animals	Food	Interesting Places	
Sports	Music	Weather or Seasons	(or others)

After everyone has a title on his paper, each student passes his paper to the person sitting on his left (or right, or however else you want to **circulate** the papers). Circulating the papers among small groups, rather than through the whole class, may give students a greater sense of ownership of their writing—and better results.

Give students several minutes to write **one** line of poetry on the paper each received from his neighbor. Each student **must** write about the topic at the top of the paper he has before him. When students have written their lines, they pass the papers once again.

Now, before students write any further, set these four rules:

1. Students must read what has been written on the paper before they write anything new.
2. They must write neatly, so others can read what they've said.
3. Each student must write something that **fits** with what has already been written. It's important not to spoil everyone's work by changing mood in the middle of a poem.
4. No rhyming is allowed. (When students rhyme, meaning often suffers.)

After students read what's been written on their new paper, they add a line of their own. Allow several minutes for this. Then have the class pass their papers once again.

Each student always passes papers to the same person and, of course, receives new papers from the same person. This may create a little confusion initially, but they'll soon get the hang of it.

Students keep passing papers and adding lines. After about eight passes, warn students that the next pass will be the final one. Then instruct them to write a line that brings the poem they have to a conclusion.

Finally, the student who writes the last line of each poem should edit and rewrite that poem. Then have students share their results with the class, by reading aloud or posting the poems on a bulletin board. Remind students that each poem is a group effort, not an individual work. Credit for a good poem belongs to everyone who contributed to it.

GA1088

DUELING POETS

For this poetry writing activity, you need an opponent (partner). Choose someone whom you will enjoy challenging, in a spirit of fun.

Poet 1, start by claiming that you are something strong and powerful. (For example, you might write "I am a great mountain," or "I am a tiger.")

_____

Now, pass the paper to your opponent.

Poet 2, think of something that will defeat Poet 1's identity. Say what you are and **how** you will defeat Poet 1's identity.

_____

_____

Pass the paper back to Poet 1.

Poet 1, claim to be something **new** that can defeat Poet 2's identity. Say what you are and how you will win.

_____

_____

Keep passing the paper between you, thinking of new identities that can defeat one another.

Poet 2: _____

_____

Poet 1: _____

_____

Poet 2: _____

_____

Poet 1: _____

_____

Poet 2: _____

_____

When your poetic battle is finished, rewrite your poem.

Be sure to ELIMINATE any errors.

ANIMAL POETRY

Let's write a poem about an animal. Choose an **interesting** animal to write about. Choose any animal in the world—common or unusual—mammal, bird, fish, insect or mollusk.

What animal did you choose?_____

Picture the animal clearly in your mind. Notice what it looks and sounds like. Notice its behavior and its surroundings. (You might even close your eyes for a minute.)

Now answer the following questions. Use plenty of descriptive details. The only rule is YOU MAY NOT RHYME.

Where is the animal?

_____

_____

What does the animal look like?

_____

_____

Describe the animal's surroundings. Use several different senses.

_____

_____

How does the animal move through its environment?

_____

_____

Describe the sounds that the animal is making.

_____

_____

How does this animal interact with the other things living in its environment?

_____

_____

Would your poem be better if the words or lines were arranged in a different order?

Make a final copy of your poem on a clean piece of paper. Do it CAREfully.

POETRY EMOTIONS

An emotion makes a great subject for a poem. Everyone has feelings, so when you write about anger or fear or joy, other people understand what you're talking about. But everyone experiences emotions differently, too. So your descriptions can be original and special.

Start by brainstorming emotions. Think of all the different feelings you can. Have someone from your class list them on the chalkboard.

Now choose one of those emotions to write a poem about.

_____

What color does this emotion remind you of? _____

Why? _____

Describe a situation when you feel that emotion.

_____

_____

What do you **do** when you have that feeling?_____

_____

Describe another situation when you feel this emotion.

_____

_____

And what do you do when you have that feeling?_____

_____

If you could do anything at all—with no limits—how would you act when you feel this way?

_____

_____

If you let yourself act that way, what would happen as a result?

_____

_____

Look back at what you've written. REARRANGE your ideas and write them in the form of a poem, on a separate sheet of paper.

GA1088

I AM A BUILDING

Imagine yourself as a building—any kind of building at all.

What kind of building would you be? _____

Now you're going to write a poem about yourself—as a building.
First, write a line that tells what kind of building you are.

_____

Now describe what you look like on the outside.

_____

_____

What do you look like inside?

_____

_____

What are you used for?

_____

_____

Describe what happens inside you or around you.

_____

_____

If you could change in some way, how would you be different?

_____

_____

Look back at what you've written. Would your poem make more sense if you rearranged what you've said?

Rewrite your poem on a clean sheet of paper.

18

GA1088

THE PERFECT PLACE

Imagine the perfect place . . . a place where you'd love to be **right now**. It might be at the ocean, at an amusement park, or beside a cool mountain stream. This is your place. You can imagine it just as you wish it to be!

Close your eyes for a minute or two and get a complete picture of your perfect place. Try to use all your senses.

Now, you're going to describe your perfect place in a poem.

First, where is your perfect place?

_____

_____

What are you doing in your perfect place?

_____

_____

What do you see as you look around you?

_____

_____

What do you hear?

_____

_____

What can you feel, or smell (or both)?

_____

_____

Describe the most special part of your imaginary place.

_____

_____

What is your wish for your perfect place?

_____

_____

Read over what you've just written. Have you chosen just the right word for each thing you want to say? As you rewrite your poem on a **clean sheet of paper**, make any changes that will make it even better.

19

SUDDENLY SMALL— SUDDENLY TALL

Suppose—just suppose—that all of a sudden you discovered that you had shrunk to a tiny size. How would you feel?

_____

_____

What wouldn't you be able to do if you were suddenly small?

_____

_____

What could you do if you were small that you can't do now?

_____

_____

Now suppose that you were enormous. All of a sudden, you've grown to a gigantic size! How would it feel to be huge?

_____

_____

What could you do now that you were suddenly very large?

_____

_____

And what wouldn't you be able to do as a giant?

_____

_____

Write a line that tells how you feel about being your very own size.

_____

_____

On a clean sheet of paper, rewrite your answers in the form of a poem.

Is there anything you can add that will make your poem even more interesting?

THE JEWEL IN THE CROWN

Sometimes all that young writers need is a seed of inspiration. And what better place to look for poetic inspiration than to the great poets themselves?

Give each of your students an isolated, intriguing line from a published poem. This is the "jewel" that they must then incorporate into a poem of their own (their "crown"). Students may use the line they are given at the beginning of their own poem, at the end, or anywhere in between. You'll be astounded at the high quality of the results.

Distribute the single lines of poetry to your students at random. You can let them "trade in" a line they don't like, but allow only one trade per customer. And don't worry if more than one student chooses the same line—because each poem that results will be very different and that will make for interesting comparisons.

Here are some lines from William Shakespeare to get you started.

The jaws of darkness do devour it up. (*A Midsummer Night's Dream,* Act I, scene 1)

Now I will believe that there are unicorns. (*The Tempest*, Act III, scene 3)

He thinks too much: such men are dangerous. (*Julius Caesar*, Act I, scene 2)

Be bloody, bold, and resolute. (*Macbeth*, Act IV, scene 1)

With silken coats, and caps, and golden rings. (*The Taming of the Shrew*, Act IV, scene 3)

I shall laugh myself to death at this puppy-headed monster. (*The Tempest*, Act II, scene 2)

The king is sickly, weak and melancholy. (*Richard III*, Act I, scene 2)

That skull had a tongue in it, and could sing once. (*Hamlet*, Act V, scene 1)

Night and silence! who is here? (*A Midsummer Night's Dream*, Act I, scene 1)

A liquid prisoner pent in walls of glass. (Sonnet V)

Pluck the keen teeth from the fierce tiger's jaws. (Sonnet XIX)

With sun and moon, with earth and sea's rich gems. (Sonnet XXI)

Like a jewel hung in ghastly night. (Sonnet XXVII)

To dry the rain on my storm-beaten face. (Sonnet XXXIV)

Of course you may want to use other lines from your favorite poets in this activity as well.

To make your sharing session more exciting, as students read their poems aloud, let classmates guess which line was the original jewel around which the rest of the poem was built.

GA1088

THE JEWEL IN THE CROWN

Your teacher has just given you a "jewel," a single line written by William Shakespeare or some other great poet.

Write that line here.

_____

_____

Your job is to set this jewel into a crown, a crown of your own poetry. Write a poem of your own. Somewhere in that poem—beginning, middle or end—you must use the line that your teacher has given you. Unless your teacher tells you otherwise, please DO NOT RHYME.

_____

_____

_____

_____

_____

_____

_____

_____

_____

_____

_____

_____

_____

_____

_____

Have you written anything that would sound better if you changed to a different word?

Make all your improvements or corrections. Then make a final copy of your work on a clean sheet of paper.

THE ROCK GARDEN GONE TO SEED

The Rock Garden Gone to Seed
By Sheldon Clamato
Newave Press, 107 pp., $17.23
Reviewed by Paul Fleisher

With this month's publication of *The Rock Garden Gone to Seed* by Newark native Sheldon Clamato, a new and even revolutionary poetry has burst upon the literary scene. In this slender volume, Clamato has welded the two divergent strains of his Japanese-Jewish heritage into a fresh form ideally suited to expressing the ironic incongruities of modern urban living (if one can call it that). Here is an example from his series on insomnia.

The neighbors quarrel.
Their screams and accusations
Pierce paper-thin walls.

Clamato calls this new form the lowku. It is a synthesis of the tingling sense of immediacy found in the traditional Japanese haiku, and the endless complaints of the frustrated city-dweller suffering in an age of alienation, decadence and bimonthly garbage pickups.

Clamato's subjects cover the full range of our social and economic woes. Yet his discomforting visions are expressed with the simple incisiveness of the traditional three line, seventeen-syllable (more or less) form.

Writing lowku is a spiritual discipline for Clamato, a means of coming to grips with the vast, conflicting forces buffeting modern man. In his poems one can sense his intimate contact with the everyday world and the deep-seated revulsion he feels toward it. This intimacy is apparent in the following lowku, chosen at random from *The Rock Garden Gone to Seed*.

In an endless line
I await the chance to pay
A parking ticket

Long elastic strands
Of pink chewing gum hold my
Shoe to the sidewalk.

She runs from the bath
To the ringing telephone.
"Sorry, wrong number."

Clamato also shows us an occasional glimpse of humor hidden behind his weary and pessimistic vision of the technological society, as in this delightful poem entitled "Boogie Down."

Snapping my fingers
I dance down the aisles
To the sound of Muzak.

GA1088

The Rock Garden Gone to Seed is not without its faults. Clamato is frequently careless about line length in his lowku; syllable counts vary from the standard seventeen, ranging from a low of eleven to a high of twenty-nine. Several other critics have found this carelessness inexcusable. Clamato has responded by pointing out that, as the creator of the lowku, he can do whatever he pleases with it. In fact, a certain sloppiness in the poems' structure reinforces Clamato's musings about overflowing dumpsters, vinyl, rude waiters and hair in the sink.

What of the apparent limitations of the lowku form? A simple seventeen-syllable verse would seem to be a poor vehicle for examining a complex industrial society in decay. And in the hands of a weaker writer, this would undoubtedly be so. But in this one small volume, Clamato has shown a master's ability to transcend the restrictions of his own chosen form, in which each word must be a carefully selected, glistening droplet of slime.

24

GA1088

LOWKU

You probably already know what a haiku is. It's a three-line, seventeen-syllable poem that captures a moment of natural beauty.

Big deal. Not everything in life is fragrant flowers and singing birds, is it? What about acid rain, mean dogs or smelly garbage cans? Shouldn't somebody write poems about them, too?

That's where lowkus come in. Lowkus are poems with the same form as haikus. They have three lines—five syllables, seven syllables, and five syllables. But they are written about less pleasant subjects. Here are some examples.

I pick up the soap.
Clotted slime covers my hand.
Faucet leaking again.

The sky is yellow
The air burns my eyes and lungs
Pollution alert.

Asparagus fern
Unwatered, broken and brown,
In a cracked clay pot.

Bang. Crash. Grind. Clatter.
5:00 a.m. garbage pickup.
It's time to wake up!

Now it's your turn! First, think of some disgusting subjects.

_____

_____

_____

Now choose the three you like best and write a three-line, seventeen-syllable lowku about each one. Have fun!

_____

_____

_____

_____

_____

_____

_____

I don't think I CARE for this at all!

POEMYSTERIES

There's so much for students to pay attention to in poetry: rhyme, rhythm, figures of speech, the sounds and patterns of words and, of course, the poet's meaning. How can you get students to notice all those things—without burdening them down with so much instruction that they'll reject the whole experience of poetry?

One way to do it is with Poemysteries. Poemysteries teach students about the structure and meaning of poetry without turning them off, because they'll think that they're solving a puzzle, not studying a poem!

What is a poemystery? Simply a poem by a professional poet that has been cut into pieces—line by line—and then shuffled out of order. The puzzle that the students must solve, working in groups of three or four, is to reassemble the poem in its original order.

Why is this a **writing** activity? Because in reassembling the poem, they must re-create a meaningful piece of poetry from an otherwise nonsensical collection of phrases.

Of course, a poemystery is much more than just a writing activity. Students must also use their reading skills. They must think critically. They must search for clues by examining punctuation, capitalization, rhyme, rhythm, word patterns, and meanings. They must evaluate possible solutions to decide which is right. And finally, they must work effectively and cooperatively with one another as their group works to solve its mystery.

Not surprisingly, solving a poemystery can take some time. Be sure to allot plenty of class time to this activity. Once students get the idea, they can work on poemysteries independently, when other assignments are completed. Students may even be sufficiently motivated to find poems that they like and turn them into mysteries for their classmates.

On the following three pages are several poems which make good mysteries. Copy them, cut them apart, and put each set of lines in an individual envelope. Save one uncut copy to use as an answer key.

But don't stop with these. Find other short poems that you particularly like. Retype them, copy them, and cut them apart to make your own poemysteries!

GA1088

The Kayak

Over the briny wave I go,

In spite of the weather, in spite of the snow.

What cares the hardy Eskimo?

In my little skiff, with paddle and lance,

I glide where the foaming billows dance.

Round me the sea birds slip and soar;

Like me, they love the ocean's roar.

Sometimes a floating iceberg gleams

Above me, with its melting streams;

Sometimes a rushing wave will fall

Down on my skiff and cover it all.

But what care I for a wave's attack?

With my paddle I right my little kayak,

And then its weight I speedily trim

And over the water away I skim.

—anonymous

The Centipede

A centipede was happy quite,

Until a frog, in fun,

Said, "Pray, which leg comes after which?"

This raised his mind to such a pitch,

He lay distracted in a ditch,

Too confused to run.

—anonymous

GA1088

Epitaph for a Horse Thief

He found a rope and picked it up,

And with it walked away.

It happened that to the other end

A horse was hitched, they say.

They took the rope and tied it up

Unto a hickory limb.

It happened that the other end

Was somehow hitched to him.

—anonymous

Mr. Nobody

I know a funny little man, as quiet as a mouse,

Who does the mischief that is done in everybody's house!

There's no one ever sees his face, and yet we all agree

That every plate we break was cracked by Mr. Nobody.

'Tis he who always tears our books, who leaves the door ajar.

He pulls the buttons from our shirts, and scatters pins afar.

That squeaking door will always squeak, for, prithee, don't you see,

We leave the oiling to be done by Mr. Nobody.

The finger marks upon the door by none of us are made.

We never leave the blinds unclosed, to let the curtains fade.

The ink we never spill; the boots that lying round you see

Are not our boots. They all belong to Mr. Nobody.

—anonymous

GA1088

The Thing That Couldn't Be Done

Somebody said that it couldn't be done.

But he, with a grin, replied

He'd never be one to say that it couldn't,

Leastways, not till he'd tried.

So he buckled right in, with a trace of a grin;

By golly, he went right to it!

He tackled that Thing that Couldn't Be Done,

And sure enough, he couldn't do it!

—anonymous

The Cats of Kilkenny

There were once two cats of Kilkenny,

Each thought there was one cat too many;

So they fought and they fit

And they scratched and they bit,

Till, excepting their nails

And the tips of their tails,

Instead of two cats, there weren't any.

—anonymous

NOT ME!

You've probably had to write an autobiography before. So we're not going to do that.

Today, you're going to write a fictional autobiography. Tell us everything about yourself—your parents, where you were born, how you spend your time, your likes and dislikes. BUT, everything you write has to be false. Don't even touch on the truth. S-t-r-e-t-c-h your imagination instead.

Don't let anyone else see your paper, either.

Now, tell us all about yourself.

_____

_____

_____

_____

_____

_____

_____

_____

_____

_____

_____

_____

_____

_____

_____

When everyone's finished, collect all the papers. Have someone read the fictional autobiographies to the class. After each one, write down your guesses about who the writer is. Once all the stories have been read, go back and reveal the identity of each writer.

GA1088

RAMBOGUS II—THE MOST EXCITING THING THAT NEVER HAPPENED TO ME

Most people your age lead very exciting lives. They've already climbed Mount Everest, won an Olympic medal, run for President, or had several hit records and a worldwide concert tour.

What? You mean **you** haven't done anything like that? How ordinary! Well then, I guess you'll just have to make something up.

Tell us about the most exciting thing that **never** happened to you. Stretch the truth until it screams for mercy! Cook up a really big one!

I'll believe you. I promise.

_____

_____

_____

_____

_____

_____

_____

_____

_____

_____

_____

_____

_____

_____

After you've finished, reread what you've written. Look for places where you can ADD more details. Details are what make a story seem real. Then rewrite your story CAREfully.

GA1088

GO AHEAD—MAKE ME LAUGH

Do you know the difference between a joke and a riddle? A riddle is a short question with a clever, funny answer. A joke is a funny story—usually much longer than a riddle. Here is an example of each.

Riddle: What word becomes shorter when the letters "er" are added to it?
The word *short*.

Joke: A man was delivering a flock of penguins to the zoo. On his way, his truck broke down. He was desperate to deliver the penguins, so he stopped a passing car.
"Listen," he said to the driver. "I'll give you a hundred dollars if you take these penguins to the zoo."
"It's a deal," the man said.
Several hours later, after his truck was fixed, the deliveryman drove to the zoo to make sure the penguins had gotten there safely. They weren't there! Frantically, the deliveryman drove around the city, looking for the man and his penguins. Finally he saw them. The man was carrying a box of popcorn.
"Hey!" the deliveryman shouted. "I gave you a hundred dollars to take those penguins to the zoo!"
"I **did** take them to the zoo," the man answered. "But we still had some money left, so I decided to take them to the movies, too."

Telling jokes and riddles isn't easy. It's important to use just the right words, in just the right order.

Now it's your turn. Tell a riddle, and a joke—in writing. Make sure you choose a joke you'll feel comfortable telling in class. If you don't know a good clean joke, someone in your family probably does. Get them to tell it to you, and then retell it in your own words.

Write your riddle here._____

_____

_____

Write your joke here. _____

_____

_____

_____

_____

_____

_____

Tell your jokes and riddles to your classmates.

TWICE UPON A TIME

You probably heard plenty of fairy tales when you were younger, stories like "Cinderella," "Little Red Riding Hood," and "The Three Little Pigs." You probably know them by heart. But, can you tell them? Let's find out.

Imagine that your younger brother or sister or cousin wants to hear a fairy tale. Choose a fairy tale that you know well to tell them. _____

_____

Now, write out the story **exactly** as you would tell it.

_____

_____

_____

_____

_____

_____

_____

_____

_____

_____

_____

_____

_____

_____

_____

Before you rewrite your final copy, read and check carefully. Have you told the **whole** story? Make sure you haven't left anything out.

When your final copy is finished, exchange your paper with a classmate. Read each other's stories, and make sure that nothing important is missing.

TALES OF TRANSFORMATION

Imagine what an interesting story it would make if you were somehow transformed into another creature! What kind of an animal would you like to become?

_____

Think of an explanation for how your transformation took place.

_____

_____

_____

What could you do as this creature that you couldn't do ordinarily?

_____

_____

_____

What would you be unable to do because of your change?

_____

_____

_____

Describe an interesting experience that you would have if you were transformed.

_____

_____

_____

_____

Figure out a way that you could be changed back to your ordinary self—if you want to.

_____

_____

_____

On a clean sheet of paper, put all these ideas together in a story.

Remember: order is important. Arrange your story CAREfully.

STORY SCRAMBLE

create a . . .
MAIN CHARACTER

Think of an interesting character for a story. The characters may be anyone or anything you can imagine—male or female, young or old, human or nonhuman. What is the name of your character?

_____

_____

In a few phrases describe your character.

_____

_____

_____

_____

create a . . .
SETTING

Try to imagine an interesting, unusual place where a story might happen. Where is your place?

_____

Close your eyes and picture this setting in your mind. In a few phrases, describe it as you pictured it.

_____

_____

_____

_____

select an . . .
OBJECT

Choose an object that might appear in a story. The object you choose might be very strange and unusual, or it might be completely ordinary.

What object did you choose?

_____

select an . . .
EMOTION or MOOD

Choose a mood or emotion that some character in a story might feel.

What mood or emotion did you choose?

_____

Now we'll turn your ideas into stories! Cut your paper along the dotted lines. Put all the pieces of paper with characters in one paper bag. Put all the settings in another bag. Put the emotions in a third bag and the objects in a fourth.

STORY SCRAMBLE, PART II

Take one slip of paper from each of the Story Scramble bags. NO PEEKING! What did you get?

Character _____

Setting _____

Emotion _____

Object _____

Now, write a story that uses all four of those things in it, somewhere! Be wacky, or strange, or even serious!

_____

_____

_____

_____

_____

_____

_____

_____

_____

_____

_____

_____

_____

_____

_____

_____

_____

Can you change anything to make your story more interesting?

After you have rewritten your stories, read them to one another and try to guess which parts of the stories came from the scrambled slips of paper.

NEWLY DISCOVERED WORK BY TOLKIEN PUBLISHED

The Houghton-Mifflin Publishing Company recently released the first copies of the late J.R.R. Tolkien's 700 page *Tarandoth Os Mifildar*, which was discovered last April by lawyers responsible for the scholar's estate. Orders from booksellers throughout the world have already exceeded the 100,000 copy first printing, despite the fact that the entire work is written in an as yet undeciphered language devised by Tolkien himself.

Apparently the author never found the time to complete a dictionary of the language. In any case, no dictionary or key has been found among his papers. Thus *Tarandoth Os Mifildar* remains, at least for the time being, totally unintelligible.

Nevertheless, the massive volume appears destined to be an instant best-seller. This is due for the most part to the enormous worldwide popularity which Tolkien's other works enjoy. However, critics who have received advance copies of the new work are already praising the discovery on its own merits. One noted critic has called *Tarandoth Os Mifildar* a "lyrical work of mystic and mysterious poetry." Another has proclaimed Tolkien a "genius whose master of the written word transcends mere meaning."

One can sense this linguistic mastery in the following brief passage, excerpted from what appears to be the fourth chapter.

Harton os banir. Na me tofarron laduna kwa misochin. Ildinfur arten bot vooris Mislindar sora. Nefil retendo. Barnoost Arillden os waadin kwa baalankor do islindar baraak, twoldur mirnath neb hanaffil seng doth.

In an effort to decipher *Tarandoth Os Mifildar*, Houghton-Mifflin has assembled some of the world's best cryptographers and instructed them to translate the book into English, no matter how long it may take. The publishing house has put the latest high-speed computer equipment at the experts' disposal, but thus far little progress has been made. In the meantime, thousands of readers will soon be delighting in the sonorous, albeit incomprehensible, prose of one of this century's best-loved authors.

GA1088

JABBERWOCKY

Rendack bazooly. Bildap napastien zu numdel weet. Alnick marpacken bund walf quinkset.

Understand? Of course not. It's complete nonsense. But playing with the sounds of nonsense words can be fun.

Can you write a paragraph made up completely of nonsense words? And can you make the sound of those words create a feeling or a mood? It's not as easy as you might think!

First, choose a mood (such as *joy, anger, sadness* or *fear*) that you want to communicate in your writing.

_____

Now, try to write a paragraph, using nonsense words that create that mood with their sounds.

_____

_____

_____

_____

_____

_____

_____

_____

_____

_____

_____

_____

_____

After your class has finished, read your paragraphs to each other. See if you can guess the mood that each writer is trying to create.

GA1088

Teacher Instructions

A SENSE OF EXCITEMENT

Sometimes it doesn't take much to trigger a young writer's imagination. Just a simple sensory stimulus can draw forth a flood of story ideas. Here's how to tap that creative stream.

First, collect a number of stimuli for your students' senses, particularly their senses of smell, touch, and hearing. Here are some suggestions.

smells: garlic, crushed pine needles, perfume, rubbing alcohol, baby powder, cinnamon or other spices, mentholated rub, peppermint extract

touch: soft brush or cotton puff on hand or cheek, drop of ice water, a puff of wind from a fan, pressure on skin from a pencil eraser or fingernail.

sounds: crumpled paper, tick of watch, door opening and closing, sandpaper rubbing on wood, bell or chime, breaking of branch or twig, shrill whistle.

Tell your students that you are going to give them a series of sensory experiences, which they must use to create a story. (Warn them which sense to pay attention to before each new stimulus.) Have them close their eyes, and let them experience one of the stimuli you have collected. As soon as they have smelled, heard or felt the stimulus, they should begin writing a story which somehow incorporates the sensation they just experienced.

Encourage students to be imaginative and divergent. Expect them to interpret their sensory experience differently. For example, one student may experience a brush on the cheek as a dog's tail; another may think of an ant crawling across her face; and a third may picture a tear trickling down.

After they have written about the first stimulus for several minutes, have them close their eyes again. Pass among the class and give them a second, different stimulus. They should then incorporate this sensation into their stories as well. Continue until the students have each experienced and written about six to eight different stimuli or until the interest level in the class seems to be waning.

Finally, have students reread what they have written. Make sure they check for places where they can change words to make their writing more precise, add ideas or details, rearrange their writing so that it makes better sense, and eliminate unnecessary ideas and language errors. Once this is done, students should write a final draft of their work.

39

GA1088

RUBBISH!

Trash cans can tell us a lot about their owners. If we know what kinds of things they use and what they throw away, we can tell about the kinds of lives they lead.

Become a trash can. Be your family's trash can, one that belongs to someone else you know, or even the garbage can of an imaginary person. Tell us everything about your owner, based on what you know from their trash and garbage.

_____

_____

_____

_____

_____

_____

_____

_____

_____

_____

_____

_____

_____

_____

"Clean up" your grammar, spelling and punctuation when you rewrite your story.

GA1088

THE GREATEST BOOK I NEVER READ

Some of the world's best books haven't been written yet.

When you write an ordinary book report, you have to read the book first. But the book you're going to report on doesn't exist. You're going to have to make it up!

As you write, use specific details. That will help your "book" come to life.

What's the title of your imaginary book?

_____

Author?_____

Publisher? _____

Describe the main character of your book.

_____

_____

Outline the story that this book tells.

_____

_____

What did you learn from reading this book?

_____

_____

What did you like best about the book?

_____

_____

_____

What would have made this book better?

_____

_____

_____

Rewrite a final copy of your book report.

ADD more details. They'll make your book seem real.

Teacher Instructions

PICK A TITLE—ANY TITLE
and
WELL BEGUN IS HALF DONE

It usually doesn't take much to get students writing, but it *does* take something. You can't just say, "OK kids, everybody write a story today." Most students need a little more stimulation than that to get started—but not a lot more. Sometimes an interesting title is enough to get them started, or an intriguing first line of a story. Once they have that, their imagination can supply the rest.

Pick a Title—Any Title, as it suggests, is a collection of titles which will stimulate students to begin writing a story. And Well Begun Is Half Done is a similar set of first lines for stories, with the same purpose. Each title or first line is printed so that the copied page can be cut up into cards.

Those titles and first line cards can be used in several ways.
—You can give a single title or a single first line to the entire class and have them all use it to write their own stories.
—You can allow each student to choose the card he or she finds most interesting and write a story based on the card of his/her choice.
—Or you can have students pick titles at random from a box and write about the ones they pick. With this method, students will often end up with cards that they do not like. If that is the case, you may want to allow them to "trade in" their cards for others, also chosen at random. However, if they decide to trade, they should then be **required** to write about the new cards. No further trading should be allowed. This forces students to seriously consider their first cards.

One interesting result of these activities is that students will develop an awareness that different people have differing ideas and viewpoints. As the class is sharing its work, it's always interesting to compare the stories of students who started with the same stimulus. Of course, their work will be quite different in style and content. And of course, that's what makes people and writing interesting.

42

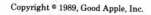

GA1088

PICK A TITLE—ANY TITLE

Dinner at the World's Worst Restaurant	The Fantastic Journey
Terror in the Night	The Boy with the Enormous Nose
Alone in the City	The Climb
The Swamp Creature	How I Became Famous
Wonder Dog Saves the Day	The Runaway Science Project
The Storm	Talk About Embarrassing!
Going for the Gold	My Brother, the Pest
The Secret Passage	The Video Kid
Visitor from Another Time and Place	Is Anyone Out There Normal?

WELL BEGUN IS HALF DONE

Cindy looked around. Nothing was familiar. She was completely lost.	"The animals have all escaped!" the zookeeper shouted.
David should never have put the small white card down. Now it was gone.	A brilliant flash of light streaked across the starlit summer sky.
She has been hungry before but never this hungry.	Mr. Williams would probably have been a pretty good teacher, if it weren't for a few annoying habits.
I awoke to a deep rumbling sound that seemed to come from the very center of the earth.	"Take it easy," the large gray squirrel said. "I don't want your whole sandwich. Just one bite."
We should never have let our father talk us into this trip.	This was the game—the game that would decide it all.
I thought all those TV characters were imaginary, until I opened my front door.	Wendy looked in the mirror and knew that it was hopeless.
The waves lapped gently against the shore, forming thin ribbons of white foam in the moonlight.	It isn't easy being the funniest guy in school.

GA1088

SO YOU THINK YOU HAVE TAX PROBLEMS?

Internal Revenue Service
Western Regional Office
San Francisco, California

Mr. K. Midas
Sutter's Mill Parkway
Eureka, California

Dear Mr. Midas,

Several irregularities in your 1985 tax return have been brought to my attention by the auditors in my department. Because of the highly unusual nature of some of your responses on the 1040 form which you filed with us, we must ask you to appear at our offices on May 17, 1987, with a complete set of your financial records for the year in question.

So that you will be able to reply to our inquiries fully, I would like to inform you of the nature of the irregularities we have found. I hope this will be helpful as you prepare to meet with us in May.

First, as you surely know, your return was filed on a sheet of heavy gold leaf which appears to be an exact replica of our Form 1040. Federal law requires that all tax returns must be filed on standard IRS forms. You certainly must appreciate that the use of nonstandard forms makes it impossible for our computers to process returns accurately and efficiently. I hope that this unusual method of filing does not signify an uncooperative attitude towards the IRS; we would look upon such behavior with great disfavor.

In addition, examination of your return shows several responses which are not acceptable for tax computation purposes. In particular, on line 31, which asks for adjusted gross income, the response "unlimited" cannot be used to compute a final tax figure. Nor can we accept without further clarification the exemption which you claim for a solid gold statue of your daughter or your $8500 deduction for jewelry polish.

Finally there is the matter of payment of your tax liabilities. You indicated that payment was to accompany your return. We have yet to receive it, although the Postal Service is currently holding several large, heavy packages which they have been unable to deliver to us due to insufficient postage.

I'm sure that when we meet in May these matters can be clarified and your 1985 return can be properly submitted and cleared. I'm eagerly awaiting the opportunity to shake your hand and to hear an explanation of your most unusual tax situation.

Ours truly,
William Greene, Senior Auditor

GA1088

FABLES FOR ALL TIMES

A fable is the simplest of stories. It is very short and has just a few simple characters, often animals. Fables may be straightforward and serious. Or, as James Thurber showed us, they can be quite humorous. And most importantly, a fable teaches a lesson, often stated at the end of the story as a proverb.

Many versions of *Aesop's Fables* and the fables of LaFontaine are available in every library. If students are unfamiliar with them, they should read and listen to them before attempting to write fables of their own. Even older students should be reminded of these classic tales before this writing exercise. Encourage students to refresh their memories by retelling a few of the tales themselves.

When students write fables, they must begin with the moral they are trying to teach. Their task is to think of a simple tale which gives an example of why that piece of wisdom is a good idea.

On the next page are some proverbs. These particular sayings have been chosen because they are simple and easy to understand and because they are less common than some others and will probably be new to most students.

These proverbs can be distributed to the students in several ways.
—Reproduce the page of proverbs, cut them into cards, and allow students to choose one at random.
—Reproduce the entire sheet, and allow each student to choose the proverb he or she likes best.
—Write a few of the proverbs on the board, and allow students to choose from that selected group.

Before they write a fable about their proverb, make sure that students understand what the proverbs are saying. Many students have difficulty with this. If yours do, give them just a very few to choose from, and spend some time discussing the meaning of each one before they begin to write.

Fables translate well into short skits. You may want to extend this activity by having groups of students write dialogue for their fables and then perform them for the rest of the class.

GA108

FABLES FOR ALL TIMES

Better to wear out than to rust out.	Hunger is the best sauce.
A cat in mittens catches no mice.	Little strokes fell great oaks.
If you would eat the fruit, you must climb the tree.	Do not run to meet your troubles halfway.
Everybody's business is nobody's business.	You can't make an omelette without breaking eggs.
There's no such thing as a free lunch.	If you would be well served, serve yourself.
Garbage in, garbage out.	If two ride a horse, one must ride behind.
No rose is without its thorn.	

47

GA1088

FABLES FOR ALL TIMES

A fable is a simple story that teaches a lesson. Fables are very short. They usually have just a few animal characters. The moral of the story, or lesson, is usually stated at the end of the story as a proverb.

Think of some of the fables you know, like the "Tortoise and the Hare." Sometimes, a character follows the wisdom of the lesson and succeeds like the tortoise. His slow and steady pace lets him win the race. And sometimes, a character learns his lesson by doing the wrong thing, like the hare. But either way, the story shows the wisdom of its message.

Try writing a fable of your own. Start with the moral. Choose a proverb as the moral for your story.

_____

Explain what the proverb means. In your own words, what lesson is it trying to teach?

_____

_____

Now, choose an animal character that suits the lesson of the proverb. (A pig could teach about greed or a squirrel about saving, for example.)

_____

Finally, write a short story in which the character follows or learns the importance of the lesson in the proverb.

_____

_____

_____

_____

_____

_____

_____

_____

_____

Remember to ELIMINATE any errors when you rewrite your fable!

BOB BUNNY MEETS THE CREATURE FROM THE BLACK LAGOON

Make a list of some of your favorite characters from myths, fairy tales, books, cartoons, or TV shows.

———————————————   ———————————————

———————————————   ———————————————

———————————————   ———————————————

———————————————   ———————————————

———————————————   ———————————————

———————————————   ———————————————

Choose two characters from your list that are very different from one another. Now, imagine what would happen if they met each other. Write a story about what would happen. Make sure your story includes:

Where, when and how they meet
What happens when they meet
What they think of each other
Any conflict the characters have, and how they handle it
An event that ends the story

———————————————————————————

———————————————————————————

———————————————————————————

———————————————————————————

———————————————————————————

———————————————————————————

———————————————————————————

Remember to ELIMINATE mistakes when you rewrite!

CAN YOU GET THERE FROM HERE?

. . . then walk down the hall about fifty feet, and take a left at the water cooler. You'll see a . . . .

It's one thing to know where a particular place is. It's a lot harder to tell someone else how to get there! Let's see how well you can do it.

First, choose a location somewhere on the school grounds—either inside or outside the school building. Choose someplace fairly far from your classroom. Write the place you've chosen here.

_____

Now, without naming the place you've selected, write an exact set of directions that will tell someone how to get there from your classroom. Write your directions on the lines below. LEAVE THE TOP LINE BLANK.

After you've written your directions, tear your paper along the dotted line. Exchange your directions with a classmate. Read the directions and see if you can figure out what to write on the top line.

. . . .

DIRECTIONS TO _____

_____

_____

_____

_____

_____

_____

_____

_____

_____

_____

_____

_____

_____

GA1088

ALIEN INSTRUCTIONAL MANUAL

Can you use a can opener, a pencil sharpener, or a door key? Of course! But what if you handed one of these objects to a visitor from another planet—and they had never seen one before?

They'd need a set of instructions, naturally! That's what you're going to do—write directions that tell an alien how to use an ordinary, everyday object.

Start by brainstorming with your classmates. List some common household objects on the chalkboard. Make sure each one has at least one or two moving parts.

Then choose one object from the list you've brainstormed. Write a set of directions that tell how to use your object. Remember, you're writing for an alien who knows **absolutely nothing** about your object. He needs every detail you can give him.

HOW TO USE A _____

_____

_____

_____

_____

_____

_____

_____

You didn't leave anything out, did you? And are all your instructions in the right order?

How good are your directions? Here's how to tell. Exchange papers with a friend. Take each other's paper home and try to follow the directions, exactly as they're written. Come back the next day and report what happened.

MONSTER EXCHANGE

Draw a monster in the space below. Let your imagination go WILD!

TOP SECRET! DON'T LET ANYONE ELSE SEE YOUR MONSTER!

52

GA1088

MONSTER EXCHANGE, PART II

On this page describe the monster you've drawn. Describe the monster **completely**. Include every detail, so that **someone who has never seen this** monster will know **exactly what it looks like.**

_____

_____

_____

_____

_____

_____

_____

HIDE YOUR DRAWING IN YOUR DESK.

Now, exchange this page with someone else in your class. Read each other's description VERY carefully. Then on plain sheets of paper, draw each other's monsters. Use ONLY the written descriptions to tell what the monsters look like.

DO NOT TALK TO ONE ANOTHER UNTIL YOU FINISH DRAWING

After everyone has finished the second drawing, take the hidden monsters out of the desks and compare. How close did you come? What does it mean if your partner's drawing looks like your original? It means you must have written a very good description!

You may want to read your descriptions to the rest of the class and then show them your drawings.

GA1088

ASK QUIZELDA

Quizelda writes an advice column in the local newspaper. Here's an example.

Dear Quizelda,
  I think I'm old enough to take care of myself. But my parents still won't let me stay home alone. How can I convince them that I'm ready to be left at home without a baby-sitter?

Mr. Responsible

Dear Mr. Responsible,
  You may feel grown up and responsible. But you still have to convince your parents. Why don't you . . .

  Sometimes Quizelda's answers are funny, and sometimes they're serious. But they're always interesting and carefully written.

  Quizelda is taking a short vacation, and the newspaper needs someone to take her place. First, write an interesting question for Quizelda to answer in the space below. You can ask about an imaginary problem or a real one.

Dear Quizelda,

_____

_____

_____

_____

_____

Signed: _____

Now EXCHANGE YOUR PAPER with a classmate. Write Quizelda's answer to your classmate's question, while he or she answers yours.

Dear _____,

_____

_____

_____

_____

_____

Sincerely,

Quizelda

EXPRESSING OPINIONS THROUGH LETTER WRITING

Students have lots of opinions on lots of subjects. When we're teaching writing, we want our students to learn to express those opinions clearly and directly and back those opinions with reasons.

Letter writing makes an ideal vehicle for practicing these skills. Good letters should be clearly reasoned, well-organized, and to the point. Of course, English teachers have to teach letter writing skills anyway. But students don't always respond well to those lessons, especially if they see them as an empty exercise in this age of electronic communication. The purpose of the next four activities is to make letter writing more than just an exercise—they're **real** communication.

People write so that others will read their words. And real letters do get read by a real audience. Students should actually send the letters they write. When students know that their letters will actually be read by the people they're writing to, they have a powerful built-in motivation to write clearly and thoughtfully and to rewrite carefully. And when the answers come back, or when a letter to the editor is printed in the local paper, the thrill that students experience is an even greater motivator for further writing.

Real letter writing also provides a built-in motivator for rewriting. Students will be more likely to get a response to their letters if they are clearly and neatly written, and error-free. Reminding students of that will encourage them to do a thorough, CAREful job of editing and revising.

Student letters **do** get responses. Not all the time, of course, but often enough to make sending them worthwhile. Newspaper editors do print letters from young people. Celebrities answer their fan mail, or at least have it answered. Companies respond to complaints or compliments from their customers, even young ones. And even most principals recognize the importance of responding to student concerns. Anyone who teaches writing should take advantage of all this responsiveness.

 GA1088

EXPRESSING YOUR OPINION— A LETTER TO THE PRINCIPAL

Your school is perfect, right? Of course it's not! No matter how good it is, everything can stand some improvement. So, make a list of some changes that your school could make to become better.

_____   _____

_____   _____

_____   _____

_____   _____

_____   _____

Go back and look at your list. Choose **one** thing that would really **make a** difference **and** could realistically be changed or improved.

Explain why you think this change is needed.

_____

_____

_____

_____

_____

_____

Explain, in detail, exactly what you think should be done to make this change or improvement.

_____

_____

_____

_____

_____

_____

Finally, on a clean sheet of paper, write these ideas in the form of a letter to your principal or school board member. Make sure your reasons are clearly stated. Don't forget to follow the proper form for letter writing and sign your letter.

This is a **real** letter. After the letter has been checked by your teacher, it will actually be delivered to the principal.

GA1088

EXPRESSING YOUR OPINION— A LETTER TO A COMPANY

Do you have a favorite breakfast cereal, soft drink, cookie, toy, or brand of clothing? Make a list of the products you like best.

_____   _____

_____   _____

_____   _____

Look at your list and pick **one** product that you would like to write a letter about.

What's special about this product? Why do you like it so much?

_____

_____

_____

When do you use this product?

_____

_____

Why do you like this particular brand, rather than other similar products from other companies?

_____

_____

_____

Make a suggestion that would make this product even better.

_____

_____

On a clean sheet of paper, use these ideas to write a letter to the company that makes your favorite product.

Address your letter to the Customer Relations Director (the person who communicates with customers who have complaints or comments). Make sure to follow the proper form for writing a friendly letter.

The company's address is probably printed on the product's packaging. If not, your local librarian can help you get it. After your teacher has checked it, mail your letter. You'll probably get an answer!

GA1088

EXPRESSING YOUR OPINION— A LETTER TO THE EDITOR

Almost every newspaper prints letters to the editor. The letters that get published are usually about subjects that have recently been in the news. Editors prefer letters about **controversial** issues—issues where there is plenty of public disagreement. A good letter to the editor focuses on only one issue. It's short, clear, expresses an opinion, and gives reasons for that opinion.

With your class, brainstorm a list of recent issues in the news. Write your ideas on the chalkboard.

After brainstorming, choose an issue that you have a strong opinion about. What issue did you choose?

_____

What is your opinion about this issue?

_____

_____

Try to think of three good reasons for your point of view.

1. _____

   _____

2. _____

   _____

3. _____

   _____

What do you think is the answer to the problem you've been discussing?

_____

_____

_____

Finally, on a clean sheet of paper, write these ideas in the form of a letter to the editor. State your opinion clearly and back it up with your reasons. Follow the proper form for letter writing. Most newspapers like you to include your phone number along with your signature.

After your teacher has checked your letter, mail it to the newspaper. You may be surprised. Student letters are printed more often than you might think.

EXPRESSING YOUR OPINION— A LETTER TO A CELEBRITY

Which TV stars, musicians, movie actors and other celebrities do you like best? Make a list of some of your favorites.

_____ _____

_____ _____

_____ _____

_____ _____

Go back and look at your list. Choose **one** person whom you would like to write to.

Explain why you chose this person. What's special about him/her?

_____

_____

_____

What has this person done that you've especially liked? What did you like about it?

_____

_____

_____

What are your special wishes or hopes for this person's career in the future?

_____

_____

_____

On a clean sheet of paper, write a letter to your favorite celebrity that tells him/her what you've said above. Make sure to follow the proper form for writing a friendly letter.

Your public library has reference books which will help you get an address for your celebrity. After your teacher has checked it, why not mail your letter. Celebrities often answer their mail. You may get a letter back!

Don't forget your return address.

GA1088

Teacher Instructions

STUDENTS AS REVIEWERS

Making judgements and committing them to paper are important critical thinking and writing skills. Unfortunately we sometimes make this process harder for our students than it need be. Let's start by letting them write about things that they are already familiar with—things they already have begun to form opinions about anyway.

Reviews of new toys or games, foods, or even TV shows make ideal vehicles for encouraging students to evaluate and express their reasoned opinions in writing. Reviews are easy to structure, they are a familiar form to many students, and they can be focused on topics that students already have knowledge and expertise about.

Reviewing a TV show is probably most appropriate for fall, after the new television season has gotten underway. Kids are going to be tuning in the new programs anyway and deciding whether or not they like them. Why not take advantage of that interest by turning it into a writing lesson?

The toy and game reviews would probably work best sometime in January—right after the holidays, when children have had a chance to try out their new playthings. Most students will be glad to bring in one of their newest toys and games from home. Or, even better, a local toy store may be willing to let your students try out some of the latest products before the holidays, in return for some good publicity such as a favorable mention in the PTA newsletter.

The restaurant review of your school cafeteria food could be done almost any time during the year. What student wouldn't relish the chance to tell the truth about the food they're served each day?

Most students are familiar with the idea of a review—they've seen Siskel and Ebert, Gene Shallit, Rex Reed, and others on television. Some may even read movie reviews in magazines and local newspapers. They already have a sense of what a professional reviewer does. This will help your students write their own reviews. You may want to spend some class time looking at some videotaped movie reviews, as well as restaurant, movie, theatre and book reviews from newspapers and magazines, before you let your students begin writing their own.

For best results, students will need ample time to use the games and toys, watch the programs or sample the lunches before they start to write. Be generous with that time! Students can't judge a TV show fairly on the basis of just one episode. At least a full hour of play with the toys and games, or even more if your schedule can spare it, will pay off in higher quality student writings. Before they begin playing, or watching, give students the review sheet that follows, so they will know what to look for as they try out the new playthings or shows.

Encourage students to choose a game or toy to play with that they have never used before. Similarly, they should choose a TV show that is new to them. And encourage students to try new and unfamiliar dishes when they review the cafeteria, too. Of course, students will also want to draw on their past experiences with other shows, games, and meals in order to make comparisons in their writing.

GA1088

OUR SCHOOL CAFETERIA— A USER'S GUIDE

Restaurant critics advise people about places where they might go out to eat. They tell readers what kind of food and service to expect. A critic should always be fair. He or she must include both the good and the bad. That way, readers learn to trust the critic's opinions.

Suppose you were reviewing the eating place you know best—the school cafeteria. What would you say? Here's your chance!

List some of the best foods that the cafeteria serves.

_____

_____

Describe in detail one dish that you recommend especially.

_____

_____

List some foods that the cafeteria doesn't prepare very well.

_____

_____

Describe in detail one dish that is particularly poor.

_____

_____

Describe the service in your cafeteria.

_____

_____

Is the cafeteria a pleasant place to eat? Describe its atmosphere.

_____

_____

What improvements should be made to make it a better eating place?

_____

_____

Rewrite your review in the form of an essay.

Everyone likes to joke about cafeteria food—but be fair.

TOY AND GAME REVIEW

Movie reviewers tell you a little bit about a movie. Then they talk about what they like and don't like about it. Finally, they give you an opinion—is it worth spending your time and money to see it?

Books, records, TV shows, and new products also get reviewed. Now you're going to write a review about a new game or toy. Why you? Think of yourself as an expert on the subject!

Before you write, read the rules or directions for the toy carefully. Then play with it until you have a good idea of what it's like.

Now you're ready to write.

Name of toy_____ Price_____

Company that produces it _____

Person who invented or designed it (if available) _____

Purpose of the game. (What is it supposed to do for people who use it?)

_____

Describe how the toy or game works.

_____

How hard is it to learn to play with it?

_____

What do you like about it? What are its best features?

_____

_____

What don't you like, or how might you change it to make it better?

_____

_____

Your recommendations: Who would like this toy or game? Is it worth the money? Is it fun? Does it keep your interest?

_____

_____

Is there anything else you want to say about the game?

_____

Rewrite your review in paragraph form.

THE NEW SEASON— WHAT'S HOT? WHAT'S NOT?

No one can watch everything on TV. That's why TV critics write reviews. They give us their opinions about which shows are good and which ones are just a waste of time. But you have opinions of your own. You know what you like, and why. Your recommendations may even help your classmates decide which new shows to watch.

Choose a new television show to watch and review.

Name of show _____

Day and time it is shown _____

Station and network it is shown on _____

Featured actors and actresses _____

_____

What is the show's setting (where it takes place)?

_____

Describe the show. What is it about? _____

_____

Compare this show with other similar ones.

_____

_____

What do you like about the show?

_____

What do you not like about it?

_____

Your recommendation: Is it worth watching? Why or why not?

_____

_____

Rewrite your review in the form of an essay.

Remember to CARE about your writing.

THE PERFECT PARENT

Wouldn't it be great to have perfect parents? Think how much easier life would be. Of course, no one is perfect—not even parents. But that doesn't mean we can't dream about the possibilities. Just imagine what the perfect parent would be like.

What would be the most important feature of a perfect parent?

_____

What would they do as a result of that quality?

_____

_____

Describe another important feature of a perfect parent.

_____

How would they show this quality?

_____

_____

Name one more important feature of a perfect parent.

_____

How would they show this quality?

_____

_____

How would a perfect parent treat you?

_____

_____

And how would you treat your perfect parent?

_____

_____

_____

REARRANGE and rewrite your ideas as a short essay.

GA1088

THE IDEAL SCHOOL

Some schools are better than others, of course. And even the best school could use a little improvement. Try to imagine the ideal school. What do you suppose it would be like?

What do you imagine the ideal school building would be like? What features would it have?

_____

_____

_____

What kinds of classes would this perfect school have?

_____

_____

_____

What special activities would the school have?

_____

_____

_____

What kinds of teaching methods would the teachers use? How would they make learning interesting?

_____

_____

_____

How would discipline be handled?

_____

_____

What part would students take in how the school was run?

_____

_____

_____

REARRANGE and rewrite your ideas as a short essay.

GA1088

RECREATION PERFECTION

Everybody likes to have fun. And what better place to have fun than a recreation center?

Suppose you were planning a new recreation center for your own community. What kinds of activities and facilities should it have?

Make a list of all the things you can think of that you'd like for **your** community recreation center.

_____   _____

_____   _____

_____   _____

_____   _____

_____   _____

_____   _____

Go back and look at your list. Some things are probably more important than others. Circle the three things that would be **most** important for **your** recreation center.

For each of the things you circled, write **at least** one reason why you think it would be one of the most important features of your recreation center.

1._____

_____

_____

2._____

_____

_____

3._____

_____

_____

Finally, on a clean sheet of paper, put all these ideas together in an essay.

Remember to organize and rearrange your thoughts so that they make the most sense.

HOW ARE YOU FEELING?

We all have emotions—feelings like anger, love, fear, hate and joy. But there are many different ways to let our emotions show. How do you show your feelings?

Choose three different emotions. Then, for each one, describe how you communicate those feelings to the other people in your life.

Emotion: _____

How I express it: _____

_____

_____

Emotion: _____

How I express it: _____

_____

_____

Emotion: _____

How I express it: _____

_____

_____

Which feelings are hard for you to show? Which are easy for you to express?

_____

_____

_____

What would you like to change about the way you show your emotions?

_____

_____

_____

On a separate sheet of paper, turn these ideas into a short essay about emotions.

Look for words you might CHANGE, so that you say exactly what you mean.

   GA1088

HAVE I GOT A DEAL FOR YOU?

Advertising copywriters have to convince people to try their products. And they have to do it in very few words, because advertising time is expensive. It's not easy, even if the product is terrific. Do you think you can do it?

Start by listing your favorite products—food, clothing, records, magazines, or anything else that you think is really worth buying.

_____   _____   _____

_____   _____   _____

_____   _____   _____

_____   _____   _____

Choose **one** product to write a 30-second radio commercial about.

Your commercial must include the following information:

___ The name of the product

___ What the product is used for

___ Why people will like the product

___ Why the product is better than similar ones

The information does **not** have to be written in that order. Your commercial must also be interesting, because you want people to pay attention!

Write your commercial here.

_____

_____

_____

_____

_____

_____

_____

   Use the checklist above to make sure your commercial includes everything it needs.

   Then time yourself as you read your commercial aloud. If it is too long, or too short, CHANGE it until it takes just 30 seconds to read.

GA1088

WKID NEWS

What's happening in your school or neighborhood? What's new?

A news story is a simple written description of an event. It should include the following elements:

— WHAT happened

— WHERE it happened

— WHEN it happened

— HOW it happened

— WHY it happened

News stories can also include a quote from someone who was involved in the event.

And if the story is about a continuing event, it should also include information about what is expected to happen in the future.

Choose an event in your school or neighborhood—something which has just happened or is about to happen.

Write a news story about that event. Check off each item on the checklist above as you include it in your article.

_____

_____

_____

_____

_____

_____

_____

_____

Do you need to REARRANGE your story so that it is clear and easy to understand?

After everyone has finished writing, put your stories together in a class news show. (You may also want to include some commercials from the Have I Got a Deal for You work sheet.) Practice reading your stories and commercials clearly. Then, if you can, put the whole broadcast on videotape.

GA1088

CLASSY COOKERY

Anyone can cook, if he/she has a recipe—a list of ingredients and a good set of instructions.

What can you cook? Think of a favorite dish that you can share with your classmates.

What's the name of the dish? _____

Make a list of **all** the ingredients you need to cook this dish. Make sure you include **how much** of each ingredient to use.

_____   _____

_____   _____

_____   _____

_____   _____

What utensils will someone need to cook this dish? Make a complete list.

_____   _____

_____   _____

_____   _____

_____   _____

Now write step-by-step directions for cooking your dish. Be careful not to leave **anything** out.

_____

_____

_____

_____

_____

_____

At home, check your recipe by actually following the directions you've written. Or exchange recipes with a classmate, and try following each other's directions.

If you discover any mistakes, correct them. If you're pleased with the results, you may want to put recipes together in a class recipe book.

LIFE ON A TROPIC ISLE

You've been marooned on a tropical island. You have everything you need to survive: shelter, water, medicine, and plenty of food. But the ship that will pick you up won't be back for a whole month. How will you spend your time?

Choose **three** items that you'd like to have with you on your island, to help you spend the time alone. Choose wisely. You don't want to die of boredom before the ship returns!

1._____

2._____

3._____

Now it's time to explain your choices. Why did you choose each of your three items? How will you use them, and why are they so important to you?

1. _____

_____

_____

_____

2. _____

_____

_____

_____

3. _____

_____

_____

_____

Finally, on a clean sheet of paper, put your ideas together in a short essay. Make sure your writing includes:
— A sentence that explains the topic you're writing about
— The objects you've chosen for your island stay
— Your reasons for choosing them

Can you guess what things your friends chose for their tropical islands?

TIME CAPSULE

One hundred years from now, historians will want to know what life was like at the end of the twentieth century. Let's send them a message—in a time capsule.

Think of five objects to put inside a time capsule that will tell future people about our lives. Make your choices carefully. We don't want to give anyone the wrong ideas about us!

_____   _____

_____   _____

_____

Now explain **why** you've chosen each item for your time capsule.

1. _____

_____

_____

2. _____

_____

_____

3. _____

_____

_____

4. _____

_____

_____

5. _____

_____

_____

Finally, on a clean sheet of paper, put your ideas together in a short essay. Make sure your writing includes:
— A sentence that explains the topic you're writing about
— The objects you've chosen for your time capsule
— Your reasons for choosing them

Make sure to ELIMINATE all grammar and spelling errors.

GA1088

MONEY TALKS

Suppose someone walked up to you, handed you some money, and said, "It's yours! Do whatever you like with it." How would you use your new-found wealth?

What you do with your money would depend on how much you were given, of course. And it would depend on what things are most important to you.

Suppose someone gave you $10. What would you do with the money and why?

_____

_____

_____

_____

Now imagine that you've been given $1000. How would you use that much money?

_____

_____

_____

_____

_____

And finally, what if someone gave you a million dollars? What would you do with all that money?

_____

_____

_____

_____

Look back. Is there anything else you want to add before you're done?

 GA1088

YOU SAID IT!

The world's writers, philosophers and speakers have provided us with a wealth of interesting and controversial quotations. Many of these sayings can serve as stimuli for student writings. Whether you're teaching history, science, literature, or even mathematics, there are hundreds of relevant quotations which will stimulate your students to think and write about important issues in that field. And usually there are quotations which take a variety of viewpoints on any issue—that makes for controversy and heightened interest among your students.

There are numerous sources for quotations, most of which are indexed by topic and author. The reference section of your local library should have several different volumes, each containing thousands of quotations on almost every subject imaginable.

To get your students writing, collect several quotations on a particular topic— preferably an issue your students have been studying recently. Write them on the board or duplicate them. Have the students choose the quotations they agree or disagree with most strongly and then explain the reasons for their choices.

More advanced students can be given individual quotations at random and then asked to explain and defend them, whether they agree with them or not.

To get you started, here are a few select quotations on two subjects from among thousands—freedom and justice.

"Better to die on one's feet than live on one's knees."—Dolores Ibarruri

"Those who expect to reap the blessings of freedom must . . . undergo the fatigue of supporting it."—Thomas Paine

"I know but one freedom, and that is the freedom of the mind."—Antoine de Saint-Exupery

"Freedom cannot be granted [given]. It must be taken."—Max Stirner

"We are not free. . . . A book of rules is placed in our cradle, and we never get rid of it until we reach our graves."—E.W. Howe

"Perfect freedom is reserved for the man who lives by his own work and in that work does what he wants to do."—R.G. Collingwood

"It is better to suffer injustice than to do it."—Ralph Waldo Emerson

"What's sauce for the goose is sauce for the gander."—anonymous

One hour doing justice is worth a hundred in prayer.—Islamic proverb

"Only the just man enjoys peace of mind."—Epicurus

Justice delayed is justice denied.—Legal axiom

"Justice must be observed, even to the lowliest."—Cicero

"Justice is truth in action."—Benjamin Disraeli

GA1088

YOU SAID IT!

Through history, men and women have said many wise, clever things about many different subjects. You may agree with some of these quotations completely. Others you may think are totally wrong.

Your teacher has given you a group of quotations about a particular subject. Choose the one that you agree with most strongly.

Which one did you choose? _____

_____

_____

Explain what the author means in this quotation—in your own words.

_____

_____

_____

_____

_____

_____

Think of some examples from real life which illustrate the idea in your quotation.

_____

_____

_____

_____

_____

_____

Why is the idea in this quotation so important?

_____

_____

_____

_____

Look back at what you've written. Rearrange your ideas so that they will make an interesting, well-organized short essay. Then write a final copy of your essay on a clean sheet of paper.

GA1088

FICTIONARY

Fictionary is a challenging, funny game. It's also a terrific creative writing activity. Students win by writing fictional definitions that sound more like the real thing than the actual definitions themselves. Fictionary works best in groups of 6-12 players, but larger groups can play too. All you need is a large dictionary and paper and pencils for each player.

RULES:

1. Choose one person as the game leader. Leadership rotates among the players after each round. Or more simply, the teacher can serve as game leader.

2. The game leader finds a word in the dictionary which he thinks no one has heard of. He announces and spells the word to the players and asks if anyone knows its meaning. If any player knows the word, another word must be chosen.

3. The leader writes the mystery word on the chalkboard or spells it aloud. The leader does **not** tell what it means or even what part of speech it is.

4. Each player writes a fictional "definition" of the word on a piece of paper. The student tries to make his/her definition sound just like a real dictionary definition. Meanwhile, the leader writes the **real** definition on a piece of paper. No one may see what anyone else is writing.

5. Students write their names on their papers, and the leader collects them.

6. The leader shuffles the papers, including the real definition among them. He then reads the definitions aloud. The players listen carefully and try to decide which definition is the real one.

7. The leader then reads through the definitions a second time. Players vote, by raising hands, for the definition they think is the real one. Each player may vote for only one definition. He may **not** vote for his own definition.

8. As he reads through the definitions, the leader records the number of votes each one gets. After everyone has voted, the leader reveals which is the real definition. He also tells who wrote each of the definitions which received votes.

9. Players score one point if they identify the real definition. They also get a point for each other person who voted for their fictional definitions.

10. Rotate to a new leader, choose another word and continue play. The player with the most points at the end of the game is the winner.

 GA1088